MEASURING MASTERS

Measuring Volume

by Martha E. H. Rustad

PEBBLE

a capstone imprint

Pebble Plus is published by Pebble
1710 Roe Crest Drive, North Mankato,
Minnesota 56003
www.mycapstone.com

Library of Congress Cataloging-in-Publication Data
Library of Congress Cataloging-in-Publication data is available on the Library of Congress website.
ISBN 978-1-9771-0368-0 (library binding)
ISBN 978-1-9771-0553-0 (paperback)
ISBN 978-1-9771-0375-8 (eBook PDF)

Editorial Credits
Michelle Parkin, editor; Elyse White, designer; Heather Mauldin, media researcher;
Laura Manthe, production specialist

Photo Credits
Capstone Studio: Karon Dubke, cover, 9, 15, 19, 21; iStockphoto: Gladiathor, cover (background), GwylanAnna, 11, NoDerog, 7, Sidekick, 17; Shutterstock: wavebreakmedia, 5, 13

Design Elements
Shutterstock: DarkPlatypus, cover

Note to Parents and Teachers

The Measuring Masters set supports national curriculum standards for mathematical practice related to measurement and data. This book describes and illustrates how to measure volume. The images support early readers in understanding the text. The repetition of words and phrases helps early readers learn new words. This book also introduces early readers to subject-specific vocabulary words, which are defined in the Glossary section. Early readers may need assistance to read some words and to use the Table of Contents, Glossary, Read More, Internet Sites, Critical Thinking Questions, and Index sections of the book.

Printed and bound in China.
970

Table of Contents

More or Less?

We are thirsty.

Mom pours us juice.

Which glass holds more?

Measure the volume to find out.

Measuring Tools

Volume measures how much space something takes up.

A measuring cup measures volume.

The lines mark the fluid ounces and cups.

Eight fluid ounces are in 1 cup (240 milliliters).

pyrex®

4 cups ▶	◀ 32 oz ▶	◀ 1 quart
3 1/2 —	— 2/3	
3 cups ▶	— 1/3	◀ 3 cups
	◀ 24 oz ▶	
2 1/2 —	— 2/3	
2 cups ▶	— 1/3	◀ 2 cups
	◀ 16 oz ▶	
1 1/2 —	— 2/3	
1 cup ▶	— 1/3	◀ 1 cup
	◀ 8 oz ▶	

We measure with cups, pints, and quarts.

Two cups are equal to one pint (0.5 liters).

Two pints make up one quart (0.9 liter).

Four quarts add up to one gallon (3.8 liters).

pint

quart

cup

We use measuring spoons

to measure small volumes.

A tablespoon is 0.5 fluid ounce (15 ml).

Three teaspoons equal one tablespoon.

Volume Examples

Dad and I are making bread dough.

We mixed flour and

two cups (473 ml) of water.

We roll out the dough.

Fresh bread will taste good.

The milk jug holds one gallon (3.8 liters).

One gallon equals 16 cups.

I drink one cup (240 ml) of milk.

There are 15 cups (3.5 liters) left in the jug.

gallon

My sister gets thirsty at her game.

She fills her water bottle.

It holds two quarts (1.9 liters) of water.

My uncle helps me paint my room.

We use two gallons (7.6 liters) of paint.

I love my new wall color.

Which glass holds more?

We pour juice into two glasses.

Each glass holds

6 fluid ounces (177 ml).

They hold the same

amount of juice.

Glossary

cup (KUHP)—a unit of measurement equal to eight fluid ounces

gallon (GAL-uhn)—a unit of measurement equal to 16 cups

measuring cup (MEZH-ur-ing KUHP)—a clear container with markings that show a liquid's volume

measuring spoon (MEZH-ur-ing SPOON)—a kitchen tool that holds a set amount

pint (PINT)—a unit of liquid measurement; one pint is equal to two cups

quart (KWORT)—a unit of liquid measurement; one quart is equal to four cups

Read More

Adamson, Thomas K. and Heather. *How Do You Measure Liquids?* A+ Books: Measure It! Mankato, Minn.: Capstone Press, 2011.

Pluckrose, Henry. *Capacity.* Math Counts. New York: Children's Press, 2018.

Reinke, Beth Bence. *Measuring Volume.* Measuring Mania. Ann Arbor, Mich.: Cherry Lake, 2014.

Internet Sites

Use FactHound to find Internet sites related to this book.

Visit *www.facthound.com*

Just type in 9781977103680 and go.

Super-cool stuff! Check out projects, games and lots more at www.capstonekids.com

Critical Thinking Questions

1. Pour a glass of water into a cup. How many ounces of water are inside?

2. You need to add two teaspoons of vanilla to your cookie batter. Should you use a measuring cup or a measuring spoon? Why?

3. If you drink two cups of milk after school, how many fluid ounces did you drink?

Index